MARINE
EXPEDITIONARY UNITS

BY NICK GORDON

BELLWETHER MEDIA · MINNEAPOLIS, MN

EPIC BOOKS are no ordinary books. They burst with intense action, high-speed heroics, and shadows of the unknown. Are you ready for an Epic adventure?

This edition first published in 2013 by Bellwether Media, Inc.

No part of this publication may be reproduced in whole or in part without written permission of the publisher. For information regarding permission, write to Bellwether Media, Inc., Attention: Permissions Department, 5357 Penn Avenue South, Minneapolis, MN 55419.

Library of Congress Cataloging-in-Publication Data

Gordon, Nick.
 Marine Expeditionary Units / by Nick Gordon.
    p. cm. – (Epic: U.S. Military)
 Includes bibliographical references and index.
 Summary: "Engaging images accompany information about Marine Expeditionary Units. The combination of high-interest subject matter and light text is intended for students in grades 2 through 7"–Provided by publisher.
 Audience: Grades 2-7.
 ISBN 978-1-60014-876-7 (hbk. : alk. paper)
 1. United States. Marine Corps–Organization–Juvenile literature. 2. Special forces (Military science)–United States–Juvenile literature. I. Title.
 VE23.G6686 2013
 359.9'63520973–dc23   2012032984

Printed in the United States of America, North Mankato, MN.

The photographs in this book are reproduced through the courtesy of the United States Department of Defense.

TABLE OF CONTENTS

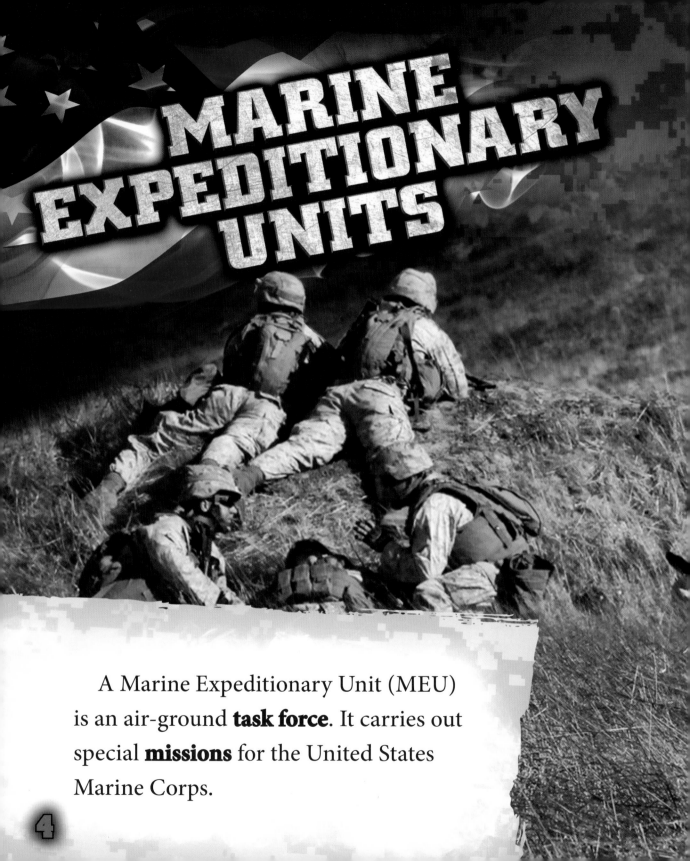

MARINE EXPEDITIONARY UNITS

A Marine Expeditionary Unit (MEU) is an air-ground **task force**. It carries out special **missions** for the United States Marine Corps.

MEU FACT

Marines pronounce
MEU "M-YOO."

The main fighting force of a MEU is the Ground Combat Element (GCE). It is often first to a battlefield.

MEU FACT

The Aviation Combat Element (ACE) provides air support to the GCE.

Founded:	**1963**
Headquarters:	**Camp Pendleton, California**
	Camp Lejeune, North Carolina
	Camp Smedley D. Butler, Japan
Motto:	*Semper Fidelis* **(Always Faithful)**
Size:	**About 2,200 personnel per unit**
Major Engagements:	**Gulf War, Afghanistan War, Iraq War, War on Terror**

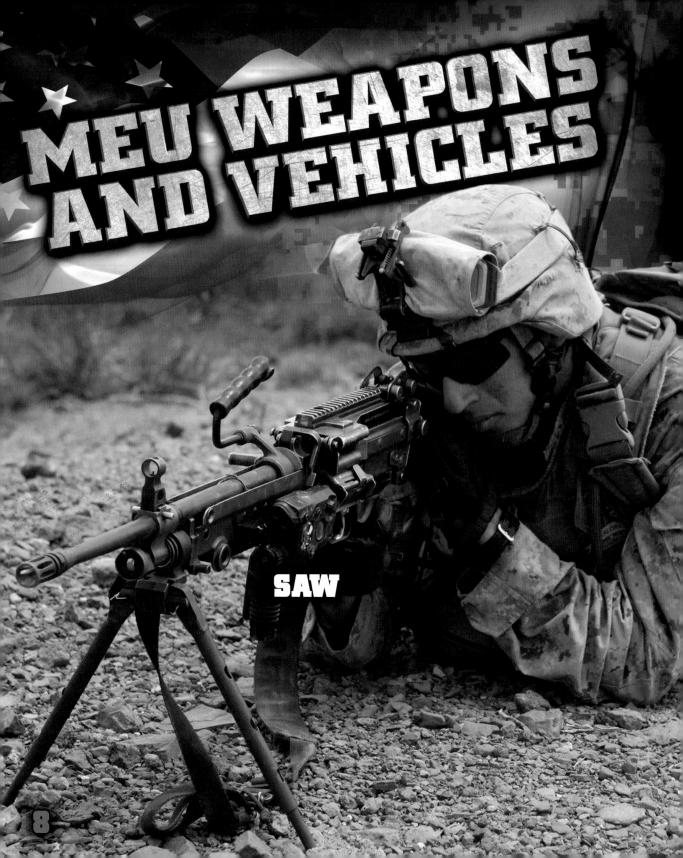

MEU WEAPONS AND VEHICLES

SAW

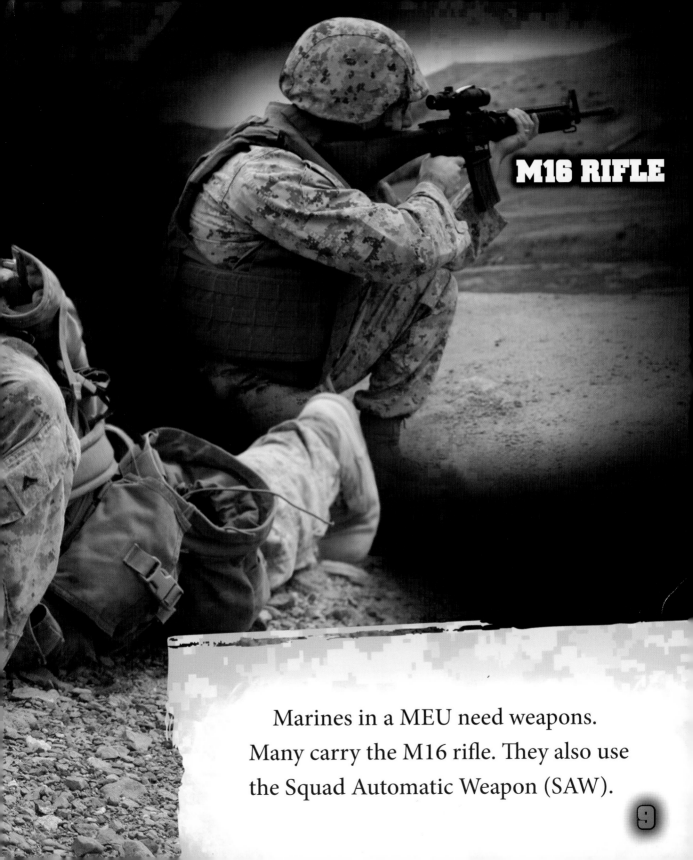

M16 RIFLE

Marines in a MEU need weapons.
Many carry the M16 rifle. They also use
the Squad Automatic Weapon (SAW).

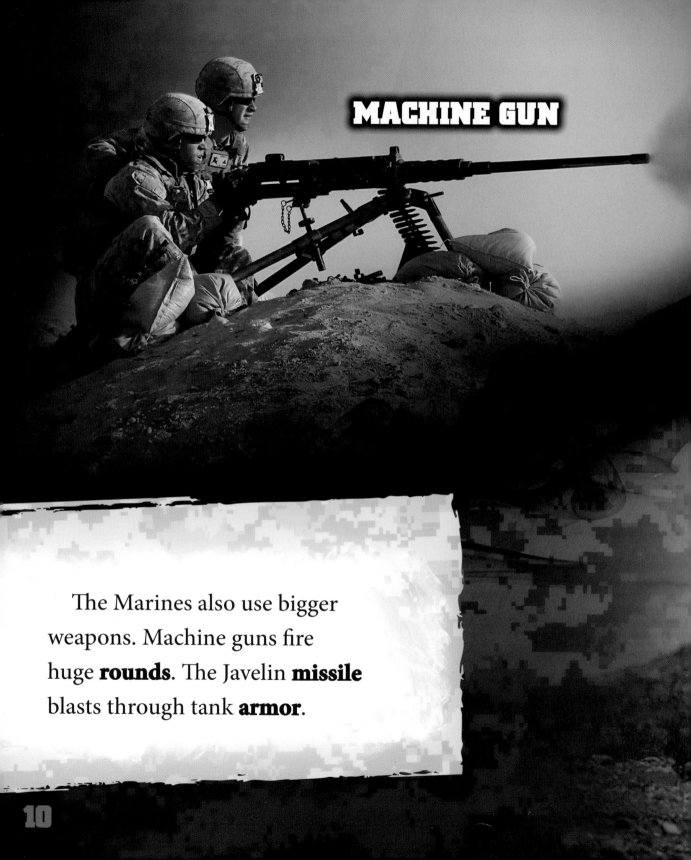

MACHINE GUN

The Marines also use bigger weapons. Machine guns fire huge **rounds**. The Javelin **missile** blasts through tank **armor**.

JAVELIN MISSILE

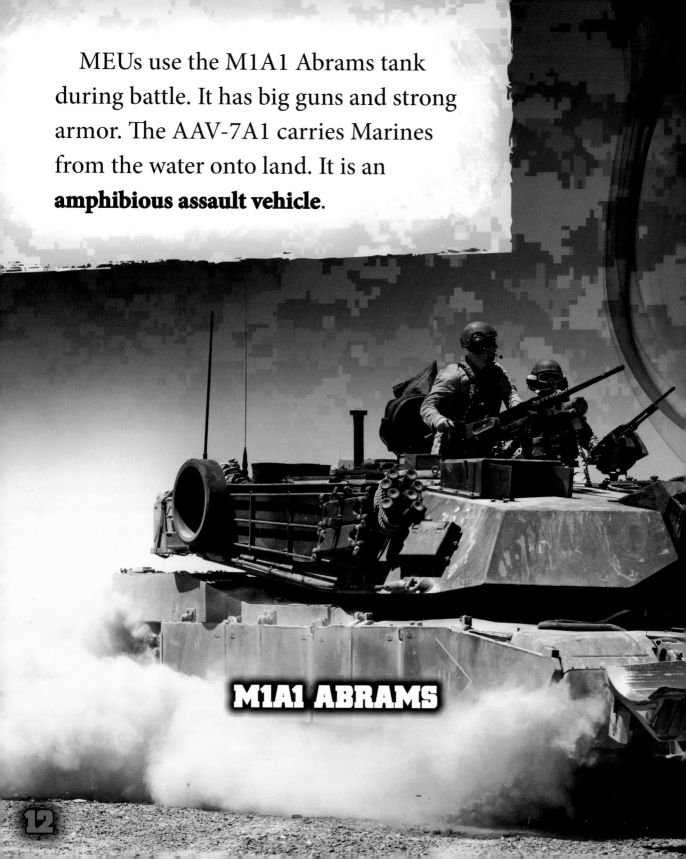

MEUs use the M1A1 Abrams tank during battle. It has big guns and strong armor. The AAV-7A1 carries Marines from the water onto land. It is an **amphibious assault vehicle**.

M1A1 ABRAMS

AAV-7A1

ATLAS

Aircraft carry MEUs to mission zones. The MV-22 Osprey can take off like a helicopter. Then it can tilt its **rotors** and fly like a plane.

MV-22 OSPREY

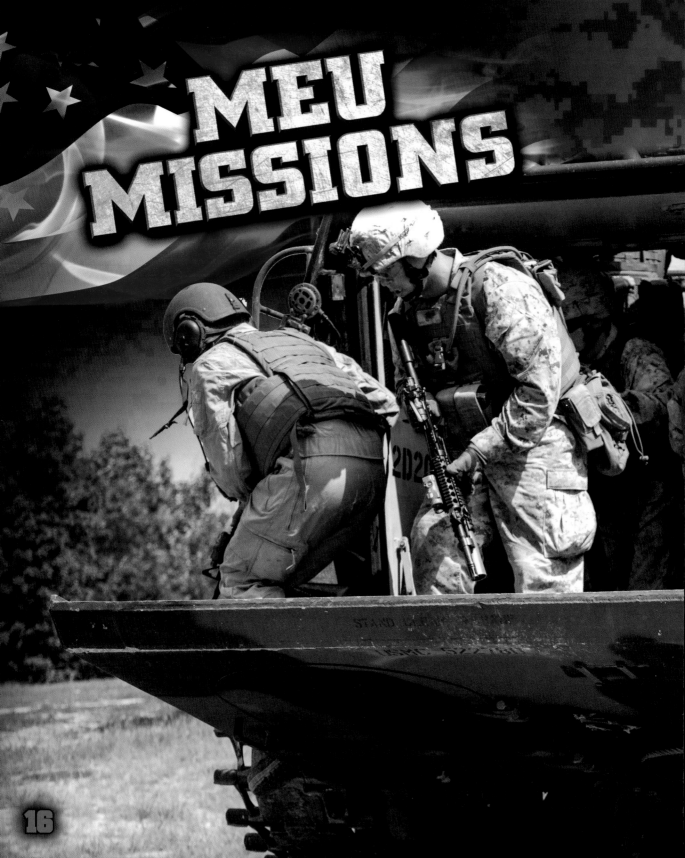

MEU MISSIONS

MEUs can **deploy** anywhere in the world in just hours. Their special missions usually involve fighting on the ground.

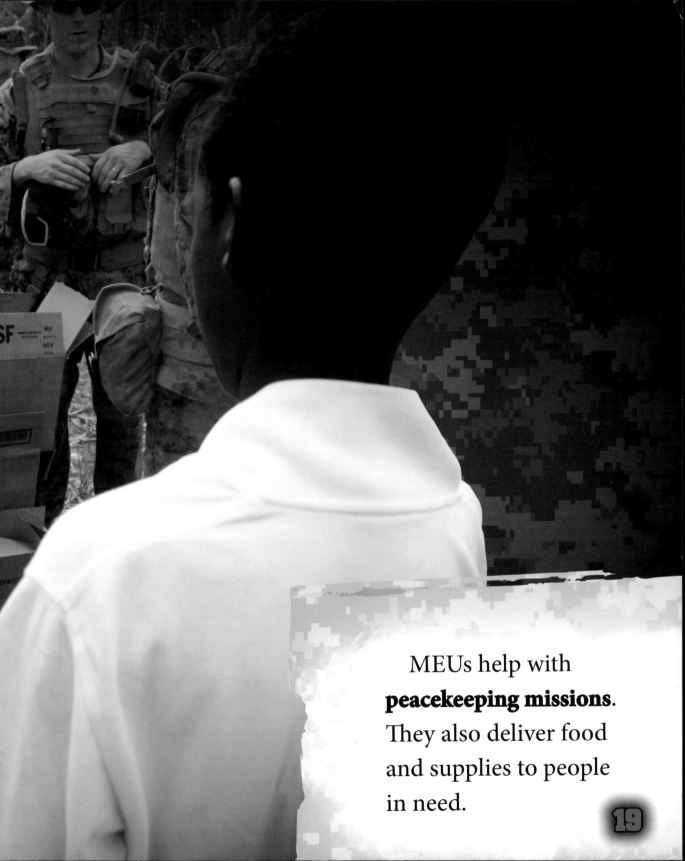

MEUs help with **peacekeeping missions**. They also deliver food and supplies to people in need.

19

Each MEU is a quick attack and aid force. Members work together to keep the United States and other countries safe.

GLOSSARY

amphibious assault vehicle—a vehicle designed to carry troops through water and on land

armor—thick plates that cover a tank to protect its crew

deploy—to be sent on a military mission

missile—an explosive that is guided to a target

missions—military tasks

peacekeeping missions—missions in which the military keeps two or more groups from fighting

rotors—the rotating parts of an aircraft that give it lift and move it forward

rounds—shots; each round has all of the parts needed to fire one shot.

task force—a small, temporary military unit formed to perform a specific mission

TO LEARN MORE

At the Library

Alvarez, Carlos. *Marine Expeditionary Units*. Minneapolis, Minn.: Bellwether Media, 2010.

Braulick, Carrie A. *The U.S. Marine Expeditionary Units*. Mankato, Minn.: Blazers, 2006.

Gordon, Nick. *U.S. Marine Corps*. Minneapolis, Minn.: Bellwether Media, 2013.

On the Web

Learning more about Marine Expeditionary Units is as easy as 1, 2, 3.

1. Go to www.factsurfer.com.

2. Enter "Marine Expeditionary Units" into the search box.

3. Click the "Surf" button and you will see a list of related Web sites.

With factsurfer.com, finding more information is just a click away.

INDEX